SECRET HISTORY

WORLD WAR II

SECRET HISTORY

WORLD WAR II

JOHN TOWNSEND

ARCTURUS

This edition first published by Arcturus Publishing
Distributed by Black Rabbit Books
P.O. Box 3263
Mankato
Minnesota MN 56002

Printed in China

Series concept: Alex Woolf
Editors: Karen Taschek and Alex Woolf
Designer: Tall Tree
Picture researcher: Alex Woolf

Library of Congress Cataloging-in-Publication Data

Townsend, John, 1955-
     World War II / John Townsend.
          p. cm. – (Secret history)
     Includes index.
        ISBN 978-1-84837-701-1 (library binding)
     1. World War, 1939-1945–Juvenile literature. I. Title.
     II. Title: World War Two. III. Title: World War 2.
     D743.7.T69 2011
     940.54–dc22
                    2010012017

SL000975US   Supplier 03 Date 0510

Pictures credits:
Corbis: cover *top left* (Melbourne Brindle/Swim Ink 2, LLC), cover *right* (Bettmann), 9 *top and bottom* (Bettmann), 10 (Bettmann), 11 (Bettmann), 18 (Bettmann), 19 (Bettmann), 20 (Bettmann), 22 (Bettmann), 23 (Bettmann), 26 (Sion Touhig/Sygma), 27 (Bettmann), 29 (Bettmann), 30 (EPA), 31 (Hulton-Deutsch Collection), 34 (Swim Ink 2, LLC), 37 (Bettmann), 38 (Hulton-Deutsch Collection), 39 (Bettmann), 41 (Wolfgang Kaehler).
Getty Images: 6 (Heinrich Hoffmann/Time & Life Pictures), 7 (Lawrence Thornton/Hulton Archive), 12 (Keystone/Hulton Archive), 13 (Keystone/Hulton Archive), 14 (Keystone/Hulton Archive), 15 (Keystone/Hulton Archive), 16 (Central Press/Hulton Archive), 17 (Keystone/Hulton Archive), 21 (Fox Photos/Hulton Archive), 28 (MPI/Hulton Archive), 32 (Keystone/Hulton Archive), 35 (Kurt Hutton/Picture Post), 36 (Galerie Bilderwelt/Hulton Archive), 42 (William Vandivert/Time & Life Pictures), 43 (Bentley Archive/Popperfoto).
NHPA: 25 (Donald Mammoser).
Rex Features: 33 (Action Press), 40 (Everett Collection).
Shutterstock: *spy camera* cover (alphacell), 24 (Sebastian Knight).

Cover illustrations: *top left*: US poster from 1942; *bottom left*: World War II–era spy camera; *right*: Serbian spy Dusko Popov (1912–1981), who worked for MI5 in World War II.

Spread heading illustrations are all from Shutterstock: 6: World War II American M24 tank (Len Green); 8, 12: World War II–era spy camera (alphacell); 10, 18, 26, 28, 34: headphones (Dmitry Naumov); 14: World War II German MP-40 submachine gun (Olemac); 16, 38: barbed wire (Nikita Rogul); 20, 22, 24: bomb (fckncg); 30, 42: World War II pistol (Wyatt Rivard); 32, 40: shovel (mmaxer); 36: megaphone (MilousSK).

Every attempt has been made to clear copyright. Should there be any inadvertent omission, please apply to the publisher for rectification.

CONTENTS

A GLOBAL CONFLICT

World War II was fought between the "Axis" countries (including Germany, Japan, and Italy) and the Allies (including the United States, Britain, France, and the Soviet Union). It lasted from 1939 to 1945 and involved 61 countries and three-quarters of the world's population. Over 25 million members of the armed forces died in the war, as well as a similar number of civilians.

German leader Adolf Hitler (1889–1945) walks up steps lined with swastika banners at a Nazi rally in 1934.

THE WAR BEGINS

World War II began when Germany, under Adolf Hitler, invaded Poland in September 1939, the latest in a series of aggressive moves by Germany against its neighbors. In response, Britain and France declared war on Germany. Italy, under Benito Mussolini, allied itself with Hitler. By mid-1940, Germany was in control of most of Western Europe.

ADOLF HITLER

Adolf Hitler and his Nazi Party took power in Germany in 1933. Hitler promised to make Germany great again, but he also had secret plans to expand German territory. He wanted to create a powerful empire that would dominate Europe and western Asia. Hitler was also a racist. He planned to enslave or get rid of peoples he thought were inferior or not "racially pure."

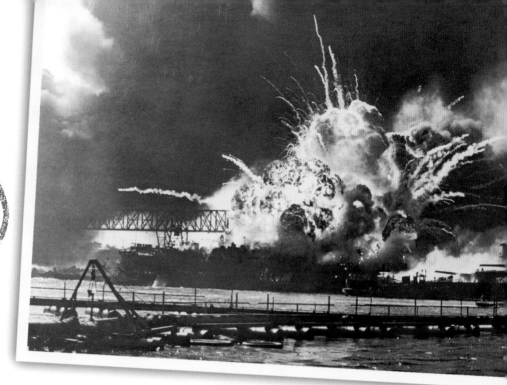

The surprise attack by Japanese bombers on the US naval base at Pearl Harbor, Hawaii, took the war to a new scale.

THE WIDENING CONFLICT

In June 1941, Germany unexpectedly invaded the Soviet Union, with whom it had earlier formed a pact. In December 1941, Japan attacked the US naval port of Pearl Harbor, bringing the United States into the conflict. The war was now global in scale.

Until mid-1942, the Axis powers won most of the battles. However, from this time, the tide of the war turned steadily against them, thanks mainly to the vast resources of the United States and Soviet Union. The war finally ended in August 1945.

WAR OF SECRETS

World War II was not just about big battles involving guns, tanks, and bombs. There was also another, secret conflict going on. Both the Axis and the Allied nations made great efforts to keep information hidden from the other side and to uncover enemy plans. They engaged in secret operations, plots, and missions to foil the enemy or take them by surprise.

IN THEIR OWN WORDS

This was a secret war, whose battles were lost or won unknown to the public; and only with difficulty is it comprehended, even now, by those outside the small high scientific circles concerned. No such warfare had ever been waged by mortal men.

Winston Churchill, *The Second World War*, Vol. 2, p. 381

SEEKING SECRETS

During World War II, many spies worked behind enemy lines trying to discover secrets. Spying was dangerous work. Those who got caught risked being tortured and shot. Even those who didn't get caught had a hard time finding accurate information, let alone getting it back home safely. Nevertheless, many people in World War II were prepared to take the risk and become spies.

GERMAN SPY IN ENGLAND

German spy Josef Jakobs parachuted into England in January 1941. However, the Home Guard saw him land and arrested him. He had forged identity papers. He also had a radio transmitter for sending secrets back to Germany.

Jakobs was interrogated in the hope that he could be made to change sides and spy for Britain. But he was a committed Nazi and refused. He was taken to a cell in the Tower of London and later shot. Jakobs was one of 15 German spies executed in Britain during World War II.

DOUBLE CROSS

MI5, the British government agency responsible for homeland security and counterintelligence, set up a secret detection center in England. Here German spies were interrogated and made to reveal their secrets. Some were trained to become double agents and sent back to Germany to find Nazi secrets. This operation was code-named Double Cross, or "XX."

Not all spying took place on the ground. During World War II, the first "spies in the sky" when powerful cameras, were used over enemy territory.

US soldiers tie a German spy to a post before executing him by firing squad. He was one of three Germans who were caught spying on Allied positions in Europe in 1945.

GERMAN SPY IN LONDON

Tyler Kent was a clerk working in the US Embassy in London at the beginning of the war. He was actually a spy who stole hundreds of secret documents and passed important information to Germany. His spying was soon discovered, and he was sent to prison for seven years.

SOVIET SPY IN JAPAN

Probably the most skillful and successful spy in World War II was Richard Sorge. Sorge was a German citizen who spied for the Soviet Union. He spent the war in Tokyo, where he posed as a newspaper reporter while sending secrets back to Moscow.

Sorge became friendly with the German ambassador so he could spy on Germany as well as Japan. He discovered that the Germans were planning to invade the Soviet Union on June 22, 1941. The Soviets, who had a pact with Germany, simply didn't believe Sorge's message and the invasion took them by surprise. In late 1941, the Japanese arrested Sorge, and he was hanged.

"Matchbox cameras" were used by OSS agents during World War II. These cameras could be hidden in an agent's hand and used to take a picture while he appeared to be lighting a cigarette.

HITLER'S SECRETS SMUGGLED TO AMERICA

Fritz Kolbe was an officer in Hitler's Foreign Ministry. He hated the Nazis so much that he copied about 2,600 secret documents and sent them to the head of the US Office of Strategic Services (OSS) in Switzerland. He didn't even want the United States to pay him for his work.

He was later described by the Central Intelligence Agency (CIA, the successor to the OSS) as one of the most important spies of the war. The information he provided included descriptions of the following:

- German plans to counter the D-day landings

- The V-1 and V-2 rocket programs (see pages 20–21)

- Details of the Messerschmitt Me 262 jet fighter

- Japanese plans in Southeast Asia

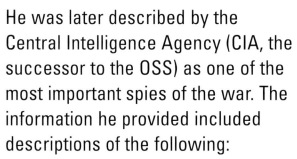

THE OSS

The US Office of Strategic Services (OSS) was founded by President Roosevelt in 1942. The OSS collected secrets about countries at war with the United States. In total, a team of 16,000 US agents worked behind enemy lines. At the end of the war, the OSS became the CIA.

WOMEN SPIES

Some of the most daring spies of World War II were women. Female spies were sometimes dropped by parachute into occupied Europe. They went as part of the Special Operations Executive (SOE), set up by the British government in 1940. By disguising themselves as peasant women, the spies would not attract suspicion and were often able to observe enemy operations and send home vital information. But they faced serious risks.

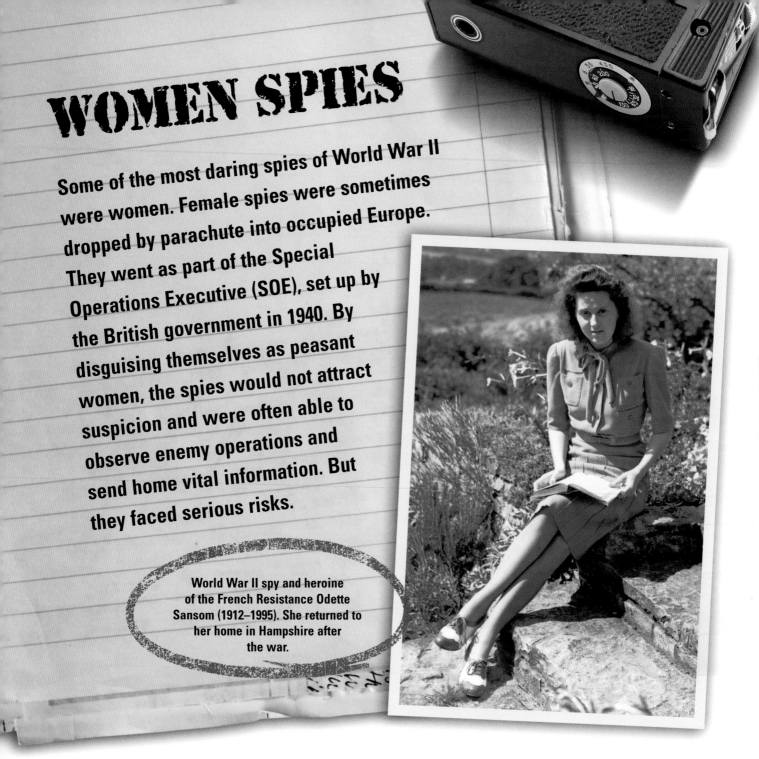

World War II spy and heroine of the French Resistance Odette Sansom (1912–1995). She returned to her home in Hampshire after the war.

ODETTE SANSOM

Odette Brailly was born in France and moved to England when she married Roy Sansom. Odette became an SOE agent and went to France in 1942 as a radio operator. In 1943, she was caught and tortured by the Gestapo (the Nazi secret police), who pulled out all her toenails to make her talk. She refused to give them any information and was condemned to death and sent to Ravensbrück concentration camp. Remarkably, she survived, and after the war, she was awarded the George Cross for bravery.

VIOLETTE SZABO

Violette Bushell was born to a French mother and English father and grew up in London. She married a soldier, Etienne Szabo, who was killed in battle in 1941. This prompted her to join the SOE. She was parachuted into France in 1944 and led a French Resistance group on secret raids sabotaging bridges. She sent back radio reports giving the locations of armament factories, which the Allies could bomb. She was eventually caught and tortured by the Gestapo. Violette was executed by firing squad. After her death, she was awarded the George Cross.

Violette Szabo was just 23 years old when she was executed. Her four-year-old daughter was presented with Violette's George Cross medal in 1946.

NOOR INAYAT KHAN

Noor Inayat Khan was a British SOE agent of Indian descent. She was the first female radio operator sent into Nazi-occupied France. Noor was betrayed by a Frenchwoman and arrested. Because she kept copies of her secret signals, the Germans were able to use Noor's radio to trick London into sending new agents—into the hands of the waiting Gestapo. Noor refused to reveal information under torture and was shot. She was awarded the George Cross.

THE FRENCH RESISTANCE

In the countries under Nazi occupation, everyone had to obey the new rulers or risk arrest—or worse. Many brave people tried to fight back against the occupiers. They joined secret organizations that carried out ambushes and acts of sabotage against the Nazis. France, in particular, had many secret resistance groups.

A group of Maquisards receive instructions before a raid. Many Maquisards received the Order of the Liberation, a medal awarded to heroes of the French Resistance during World War II.

THE MAQUIS

In France, many of the groups that were determined to resist the invaders hid in the forests and the countryside. They began to organize themselves into a resistance movement called the Maquis—a name for the bushes they used when hiding from the Germans.

As the Maquis groups grew, they led attacks on German forces. They aided the escape of Jews, communists, and others who the Gestapo were determined to hunt down. Maquisards also helped many of the spies working secretly in France. When British and US pilots were shot down over France, the Maquis helped them return to Britain.

OPERATION JEDBURGH

British and US secret agents parachuted into France to support the work of the French Resistance. They ran sabotage missions against the Germans, helped by local Maquis groups. The "Jeds" as they were called (they trained in the town of Jedburgh in Scotland) were sometimes caught and tortured.

Telephone operators helped members of the Maquis, who used a special code to report the movements of German forces in France.

REVENGE

Allied forces invaded Normandy in June 1944 (D-day) and Provence in August. Before these attacks, the Allies transmitted coded messages to the French Resistance asking them to target German garrisons. These undercover attacks greatly helped the rapid Allied advance through France.

However, there was a cost. In revenge for the French attacks, the Nazis hanged 120 men in Tulle. A German major also ordered the execution of more than 600 men, women, and children before setting fire to a village. Despite this, the French Resistance continued their dangerous work until the end of the war.

GILBERT RENAULT

A famous secret agent of the French Resistance was Gilbert Renault, known as Colonel Rémy. He passed Nazi secrets to Britain, which helped the Allied forces prepare for their invasion of France. Awarded the Order of the Liberation medal in 1942, he was on the Gestapo's "wanted list" but was never captured.

SECRET POLICE

Dictators can only rule with the help of a large and powerful secret police force to hunt down, imprison, or kill opponents of their regime. Hitler's secret state police was called the Gestapo, and its ruthless methods spread fear wherever the Nazis went. The Gestapo was founded in 1933 by Hermann Goering and was later led by Heinrich Himmler.

Heinrich Himmler (1900–1945) was head of the SS. His goal was to kill all the Jews in Europe.

THE GESTAPO

During World War II, the Gestapo followed the advancing German army as part of the SS, Hitler's vast army of henchmen and bodyguards. Once German rule was established, the Gestapo would round up those they regarded as enemies, including communists, Jews, and anyone who resisted Nazi rule. Thousands were imprisoned or shot without trial.

IN THEIR OWN WORDS

Pastor Harald Sandbaek, a leader of the Danish resistance, describes being tortured by the Gestapo in October 1944:

I declared that I had no more to say, after which those devils handed me over to the torturers. They half dragged and half carried me up to the attic of the college, took off all my clothes, and put on new handcuffs. To these a string was attached which could be tightened and caused insufferable pain. I was thrown on a bed and whipped with a leather dog whip.

Quoted in Spartacus Educational:
www.spartacus.schoolnet.co.uk/GERgestapo.htm

The Gestapo used brutal methods such as electric shocks, beatings, or near drowning in bathtubs filled with ice-cold water to make people confess their secrets. They had about 45,000 members but had another 160,000 agents and informers. People in occupied Europe had to be careful not to say or do anything that might arouse suspicion in case someone reported them to the Gestapo.

The Gestapo arrested many thousands of innocent people, like this group of Jewish men hiding in a cellar in Poland.

ITALY'S SECRET POLICE

The secret police in Mussolini's Italy was called the OVRA. Though hated by many, the OVRA was not as ruthless as the Gestapo. One method they used to stop troublemakers was to tie them to a tree and make them drink castor oil before forcing them to eat a live toad.

JAPAN'S SECRET POLICE

In World War II, Japan's military police were the Kempeitai. Their job was to maintain security in the Japanese homeland and in the many Japanese prisoner-of-war camps scattered around Southeast Asia. The Kempeitai was notorious for its brutality and frequent use of torture against prisoners and civilians suspected of crimes against the state.

SECRET WEAPONS: INVISIBLE WAVES

During World War II, each side competed to develop weapons and equipment that would give them a decisive advantage over their enemies. Large teams of top scientists were recruited to come up with ever more deadly weapons—many of them quite bizarre.

This station on Britain's east coast was part of the world's first radar system. It was used during World War II to detect incoming enemy aircraft.

RADIO WAVES

Radar (*r*adio *d*etection *a*nd *r*anging) was a new technique for working out the position and movement of an object by measuring radio waves reflected from its surface. Radar was first developed in Britain in the 1930s, and the British government soon realized the technology had military applications.

Radar played a vital role during the Battle of Britain (July–October 1940). A chain of radar stations along the English coast gave early warning of German aircraft crossing the English Channel

MINIATURE RADAR

By 1940, radar technology had advanced to the point where very small objects could be detected from long distances. Small radar antennae on Allied bombers greatly improved the accuracy of bombing raids on German cities. Aircraft could now detect objects as small as a submarine periscope, allowing ships or bombers to attack and destroy previously undetectable German submarines.

Radar operators on board ships could pick up vital information, as on this aircraft carrier in the Pacific during strikes against Japan.

and North Sea. This gave the Royal Air Force (RAF) time to send up fighter planes to attack the approaching bombers.

BATTLE OF THE BEAMS

German aircraft used radio signals to locate targets in Britain for night bombing. They beamed two radio signals to form a cross above a target. Bomber pilots flew along one beam and as soon as they picked up the other signal, they dropped their bombs. This accurate bombing caused great damage to British cities, factories, and military installations.

The British fought back by transmitting other radio signals to confuse the pilots. The Germans had to develop a different system of radio signals to direct their bombers. The British used spies and interrogated captured German pilots to find out how this worked. They were then able to beam yet more radio signals at advancing aircraft, causing them to miss their targets.

R. V. JONES

Reginald Victor (R. V.) Jones was a British scientist who played a crucial role in the Battle of the Beams. On Jones's advice, the British began to counter the German radio signals with their own. Jones also suggested that pieces of metal foil falling through the air would create radar echoes and confuse the enemy. These falling clouds of foil became known as "chaff."

19

SECRET WEAPONS: HITLER'S MISSILES

By 1941, Nazi leaders were becoming concerned about the rising losses of German planes and pilots on air raids over British cities. They were determined to reduce their losses, so German scientists began secret work to develop long-range pilotless rocket bombs.

DOODLEBUGS

The first version of the pilotless rocket bomb, known as the V-1, carried a 1,880-pound (850-kilogram) warhead and was powered by a jet engine. It traveled at 350 miles per hour (560 kilometers per hour) and had a range of 150 miles (240 kilometers). Nearly 10,000 of these "doodlebugs'" were fired at Britain from northern France, killing over 6,000 people.

THE FIRST MODERN ROCKET

In September 1944, a V-2 rocket was fired at London. These missiles, built by the Nazis using slave labor, were powered by liquid fuel and provided the model for all future rockets. The V-2 had a 2,166-pound

A German V-1 "doodlebug" flying bomb falls on a town in southern England in June 1944.

(980-kilogram) warhead and a speed of 2,480 miles per hour (4,000 kilometers per hour). Their mobile launchpads made it difficult for Allied bombers to detect and destroy them before they were in the air. Over 3,000 were launched at various Allied targets, killing over 7,000 civilians.

THE V-3 CANNON

The Germans also developed the V-3, an underground cannon, capable of firing shells at London from giant bunkers in northern France. The V-3 would have been able to fire 300 shells an hour at a speed of one mile (1,500 meters) per second. But the project was abandoned when Allied troops captured it after D-day.

The German V-2 long-range missile was the forerunner of modern space rockets.

MIRACLE WEAPONS

At the end of World War II, US special intelligence units searched German factories to find Hitler's secret weapon plans. They found designs for many advanced weapons, from a gun that could shoot a stream of metal at five miles (8,000 meters) per second to an orbiting solar mirror gun. Hitler had hoped that these *Wunderwaffen* ("miracle weapons") would stop the advancing Allies in their tracks—but he ran out of time.

IN THEIR OWN WORDS

After the war, aeronautical engineer Roy Fedden led a fact-finding tour of secret Nazi research facilities on behalf of the British government. He reported:

I have seen enough of their designs and production plans to realize that if they [the Germans] had managed to prolong the war some months longer, we would have been confronted with a set of entirely new and deadly developments in air warfare.

Quoted on www.burlingtonnews.net/hitlersufo.html

21

SECRET WEAPONS: THE BOMB

From 1942, US scientists worked in secret to create a bomb so powerful it could end the war. The bomb's explosive power would come through the release of energy stored within atoms. Fear that the Germans would master the technology first drove the scientists on.

American scientist Robert Oppenheimer, leader of the Manhattan Project, views the remains of the steel tower, which melted in the intense heat where the first atomic bomb was tested.

SPLITTING THE ATOM

In the early 20th century, the great physicist Albert Einstein (1879–1955) showed that matter could be turned into energy. To do this, scientists had to split the basic building blocks of matter—atoms. At the center of every atom is a cluster of particles called the nucleus. Splitting the nucleus could release tremendous amounts of energy—known as nuclear energy.

Thousands of people were involved in the "Manhattan Project" to build the bomb.

IN THEIR OWN WORDS

In August 1939, Albert Einstein wrote to President Franklin Delano Roosevelt about the possibility of making a massive "atom bomb":

A single bomb of this type, carried by boat or exploded in a port, might very well destroy the whole port together with some of the surrounding territory.

From Kim Philby, *My Silent War* (MacGibbon & Kee, 1968)

A mushroom cloud towers more than 3.7 miles (six kilometers) above Nagasaki following the nuclear attack by the United States. The heat on the ground reached about 5,400 degrees Fahrenheit (3,000 degrees Celsius).

CHAIN REACTION

Scientists call splitting the atom "nuclear fission." The scientists of the Manhattan Project aimed to create a fission chain reaction. When one atom was split, the particles given off would split the nuclei of other atoms, which would split still others. The chain reaction could only be achieved by using certain rare forms of radioactive elements such as uranium and plutonium. *Radioactive* means elements emit energy in the form of streams of particles.

On July 16, 1945, after three years' research, they produced the world's first nuclear explosion. It was equivalent to 20,900 tons (19,000 metric tons) of TNT and it threw into the sky a mushroom-shaped cloud of vapor and debris.

HIROSHIMA AND NAGASAKI

Soon afterward, the United States used nuclear bombs for the first time as weapons of war. Victory was imminent in the United States' war against Japan, but the Japanese refused to surrender, and an invasion looked like the only solution. This was likely to cost the lives of hundreds of thousands of soldiers and civilians.

The US government decided instead to drop nuclear bombs on two Japanese cities to convince the Japanese to surrender. "Little Boy" was dropped on Hiroshima on August 6, 1945, leveling two-thirds of the city and killing about 200,000. Three days later, "Fat Man" was dropped on Nagasaki. Japan surrendered on September 2, ending World War II.

SECRET WEAPONS: RISKY AND RIDICULOUS

Not all secret weapons in World War II used the latest science and technology. Some were simply bizarre and not very friendly to animals.

ANTI-TANK DOGS

The Soviet Union trained dogs to carry bombs on their backs and to run under enemy tanks. As the dog slid under a tank, a lever sticking up from the dog's back would switch on the bomb. The enemy tank, as well as the dog, would be destroyed.

The Soviet dog trainers kept the dogs hungry and taught them to run under tanks to find food. But there was a problem. In their training, the dogs were fed under Soviet tanks, not German tanks, which looked different. So during

DUMMY LOGS

The British came up with a secret container for carrying grenades— a pretend log! The plaster logs were used for smuggling ammunition into enemy territory. Sealed containers were built into the logs, which were carefully made to look very real. The only danger was if someone tried to burn one on a log fire!

battles, the dogs tended to run under the Soviet tanks and blow *them* up! However, in one battle, dogs were reported to have destroyed 12 German tanks.

BAT BOMBS

An American dentist came up with an idea for getting back at Japan for bombing Pearl Harbor. He suggested strapping small firebombs to thousands of bats and dropping them over Japan. The bats would roost inside buildings during the day, and then timers would ignite the bombs. Thousands of Japanese buildings would be destroyed. That was the theory!

The US Navy carried out tests with thousands of bats. In one episode during testing, a colony of bats with bombs escaped and roosted under a fuel tank at an air base in New Mexico. The resulting fire caused extensive damage. The project was dropped soon afterward.

EXPLODING RATS

It was Britain's Special Operations Executive that came up with the idea. Why not, they suggested, use dead rats packed with explosives to blow up the enemy's boilers? The idea was to leave "rat bombs" on piles of coal. When they were shoveled into the boiler along with the coal, the heat would detonate the bombs. In fact, the rat bombs were never used. The Germans discovered the first batch and the secret was out!

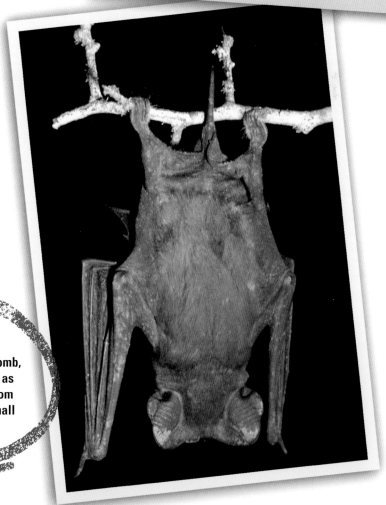

Mexican free-tailed bats such as this one were to be used in the proposed bat bombs. The inventor of the bomb, Dr. Lytle Adams, predicted they would be as effective but less devastating than the atom bomb. They would cause thousands of small fires across the target city, yet little loss of life.

25

CODES AND CODE BREAKERS

In wartime, governments and armed forces must often share secret information about plans and operations. The challenge is to keep these communications secret from the enemy. This is usually done by putting confidential information into code, making it meaningless to anyone without a code breaker.

The Enigma machine contained many cogs and wheels, which could be set in different ways. Each setting produced a unique set of coded letters.

ENIGMA

In World War II, the Germans used a very advanced code machine called Enigma. The machine encoded all communications sent from military headquarters to outposts in occupied Europe. Enigma used a series of rotating wheels to scramble messages into meaningless text. It contained billions of possible combinations, so if you didn't

CODES IN TOOTHPASTE

Spies had to find ways of carrying and hiding secret codes. That could mean stitching paper into clothes or hiding messages inside everyday objects. Toothpaste tubes were often used. The top would be filled with toothpaste, but underneath, there would be a space to hide a message.

know the Enigma setting, the message was impossible to figure out. To make things even harder, the code's settings were changed every day.

CRACKING THE CODE

At the start of the war, the British set up a team of expert code breakers to try to crack the Enigma code. They were based at "Station X" in Bletchley Park, Buckinghamshire. The initial team of four had risen to about 3,500 by the end of 1942, and about 9,000 by January 1945.

The Germans, with their orderly way of doing things, actually helped the code breakers since coded messages would often start with the words *To the Group*. Such repeated phrases were known as cribs and were a great help in cracking other parts of the code. The code breakers were also helped by the fact that no letter could be coded as itself, reducing the number of possible settings for Enigma. Using these clues, the code breakers succeeded in cracking the code on many occasions.

CODE TALKERS

In the Pacific war between the United States and Japan, the US Marines frequently used Native Americans to send secret messages by radio or telephone. While ordinary codes can be broken fairly quickly, codes based on a unique language must be studied for a long time before being understood. The Japanese never cracked the spoken code. US commanders claim the United States would never have won the Battle of Iwo Jima without the help of the "code talkers."

Two US Marine "code talkers" use their native Navajo language to send a radio signal during a battle in the Pacific war.

SECRET INTELLIGENCE

The information decoded by the Allies at Bletchley Park and elsewhere was known as Ultra. The Allies were able to use Ultra to prepare for or evade enemy attacks and to launch attacks of their own. This secret intelligence undoubtedly helped the Allies win the war.

THE WAR IN EUROPE

Ultra provided the British with information about Operation Sea Lion, the planned German invasion of Britain. It also helped the British during the Battle of Britain, guiding them on how best to deploy the fighter planes of the RAF.

Just after the D-day landings, decoded signals between Hitler and his generals helped Allied forces in Europe. The messages revealed when German reserve forces might be committed to battle.

BATTLE OF THE ATLANTIC

Perhaps the greatest triumph of the Bletchley Park code breakers was cracking Naval Enigma, the code used by the German U-boats (submarines) in the North Atlantic. The U-boats were sinking large numbers of Allied ships, threatening vital supplies to Britain.

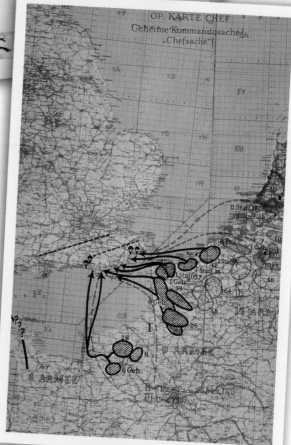

A secret map of 1941 with details of Operation Sea Lion, the planned invasion of Britain by the Germans.

D-DAY DECEPTIONS

The Allied invasion of Europe was a huge undertaking that somehow had to be kept secret from the Germans. Much effort went into deception activities so that the Germans would not know the exact timing and location of the landings. These involved the use of dummy tanks, fake ships, and elaborate troop movements. Ultra intelligence reassured the Allies that these deceptions were working.

Just after this German U-boat surfaced, it was sunk by US bombers as a result of decoded secret intelligence.

The decoded messages enabled the Allies to work out the routes of U-boat patrols, and ships could then be rerouted to evade them. Historians estimate that cracking Germany's Naval Enigma shortened the war by more than a year.

COVERING THEIR TRACKS

A key challenge for the Allies was to ensure that Germans did not find out that their codes had been broken. Otherwise, the Germans might use even more complex codes. The Allies therefore took care to cover their tracks. For example, before an attack on a ship, they would send out a scout plane, making sure the Germans spotted it. The Germans would then think it was the plane and not a code breaker that was responsible for the attack that followed.

"CONGRATULATIONS, MR. X"

The Allies were able to decode messages sent by the Germans detailing the course of ships carrying supplies from Europe to troops in North Africa. When a convoy of ships from Naples in Italy was attacked and sunk by Allied aircraft, the Germans grew suspicious. So Allied commanders sent a message to a spy in Naples congratulating him on his excellent work. As planned, the Germans intercepted this message and believed it. The spy, however, did not exist.

SECRET PLOTS

By mid-1943, the tide of the war had turned against Germany. Some officers in the German army privately began to question Hitler's judgment. They regarded him as the person responsible for the disaster facing their country. They held secret meetings to decide what to do. They knew that if word got out about their plots, they would be killed, along with their families.

GETTING RID OF HITLER

The plotters believed that assassinating Hitler was the only way to save Germany. A new government could then be formed and a peace negotiated with the Western Allies in time to prevent Germany from being invaded by the Soviet Union.

OPERATION VALKYRIE

The most serious plot to kill Hitler was called Operation Valkyrie, and it took place on July 20, 1944. On that date, Hitler met with senior army officers at his Wolf's Lair military headquarters on the Eastern Front. One of the officers in attendance was Claus von Stauffenberg, a leading member of the plot. He came to the meeting with a time bomb in his briefcase.

Claus von Stauffenberg
(1907–1944) was a supporter of Hitler at the start of the war. He is now remembered as a tragic hero who could have shortened the war if his plot had succeeded.

PLOTS AGAINST HITLER

There were several attempts to kill Hitler. In 1943, a bomb was placed on an airplane with Hitler on board, but it failed to go off. A few days later, a suicide bomber tried to kill Hitler at an exhibition of captured Soviet weapons—but the dictator left the exhibition early. Other attempts were made using grenades and guns, but luck favored Hitler every time.

Adolf Hitler shows Italian dictator Benito Mussolini his damaged Wolf's Lair headquarters after the bomb blast that nearly killed him on July 20, 1944.

He placed the briefcase under the conference table. After a few minutes, he made an excuse and left the room. Soon afterward, the bomb detonated. The room was demolished and four people were killed. Hitler, however, was shielded from the blast by a thick table leg, and he survived with only minor injuries.

THE PLOTTERS' FATE

Stauffenberg and the other plotters believed Hitler was dead, and they prepared to take over the government in Berlin. Meanwhile, Hitler quickly ordered that Stauffenberg be shot by a firing squad. Eight of the other plotters were also executed. Their hangings were filmed and shown to Hitler.

THE PLOT TO KILL CHURCHILL

In 1943, the Germans managed to obtain details of the route to be taken by British prime minister Winston Churchill on a flight home from Egypt. The plane would stop at Algiers and Gibraltar on its way to London. Four Nazi assassins were sent to North Africa with orders to kill him when his plane landed there. However, code breakers at Bletchley Park learned of the plot, so Churchill changed his flight plan.

ESCAPES

Many people spent the war imprisoned by the enemy. They included thousands of ordinary civilians in Japanese-controlled Southeast Asia as well as captured soldiers, airmen, and political opponents in Nazi-occupied Europe. Some prisoners of war (POWs) decided to risk all and try to escape. Failure usually meant death, so any escape attempt required immense courage, careful planning, and great secrecy.

Captured RAF officers at Stalag Luft III lay the foundations for a new hut. From here, 76 POWs made a break for freedom, inspiring the war movie *The Great Escape*.

STALAG LUFT III

One of the most famous escapes of World War II was the mass breakout of Allied POWs from the German prison camp Stalag Luft III in Poland. The Nazis considered the camp escape proof. However, the prisoners had other ideas and decided to tunnel their way out. They built three tunnels, 30 feet (nine meters)

THE ONLY GERMAN TO ESCAPE

Franz von Werra (1914–1941) was a German fighter pilot who was shot down over England. He was captured and sent to a prison in Canada. He managed to escape from there and crossed the United States to Mexico. On his return to Germany, Hitler awarded him a medal. Seven months later, Werra's aircraft disappeared over the North Sea. His body was never recovered.

deep and about 330 feet (100 meters) long. Out of odd bits of equipment, they fashioned pumps to feed air to the tunnelers and railcar systems for removing sand from the tunnels. They even installed electric lighting.

TUNNELING TO FREEDOM

Somehow, the prisoners at Stalag Luft III managed to keep their operation secret. When German guards eventually discovered one of the tunnels, the operation appeared doomed. But another of the tunnels was completed soon afterward and on March 24, 1944, 76 prisoners escaped. However, only three of them managed to evade recapture and get back home.

RAID AT LOS BAÑOS

There were few escape attempts from Japanese POW camps because of the high security and brutality of the regimes there. However, US and Filipino forces did launch a spectacular raid on a Japanese camp at Los Baños in the Philippines. The raid took place on February 23, 1945. It relied on stealth, speed and surprise and was an outstanding success, resulting in the liberation of over 2,000 POWs and internees. When they found out what had happened, the Japanese soldiers turned their anger on the local population, killing some 1,500 men, women, and children.

KEEPING QUIET

Life was tough for civilians on the home front during World War II. Many lived in fear of air raids and had to cope with shortages of food and other essentials. Children were often evacuated to places in the countryside, far from their parents. People also had to live in a world of secrets.

LIMITED NEWS

Unlike today, the news media gave very few details of important events. It was considered safer and better for everyone if no one knew exactly what was going on.

CARELESS TALK...

Civilians were told to be careful about passing on information to anyone. Posters warned people not to gossip since "careless talk costs lives." Servicemen and -women

Posters warning of the danger of "saying too much" were probably exaggerated, but they helped to make the public aware of security matters and feel they were part of the war effort.

REMOVING NAMES

In 1939, while the threat of a Nazi invasion hung over Britain, the government ordered signposts across the country to be painted over or removed. They wanted to make it harder for invading forces to find their way around. They also feared that low-flying German aircraft would be able to navigate by seeing place names. Railway station names were taken down, and everyone was warned not to give strangers directions in case they were enemies or spies.

This posed photo from 1943 aimed to show the British public how to spot a Nazi spy in a pub. Conditions in Germany were apparently so bad by this time that the coat of the "spy" (on the left) would be worn and thin, the buttons broken and the shoulders unpadded.

were forbidden to tell their families what they were doing and where, just in case the enemy found out. Letters to and from loved ones serving on the front were censored, and any sensitive information was removed. The motto was "secrets save lives."

HIDING BAD NEWS

During World War II, governments wanted to keep bad news hidden because they feared its effects on national morale. Censorship was used to hide the truth from citizens as much as to hide it from the enemy.

THE ROHNA

In 1943, a German missile sank the British troopship *Rohna* off the coast of Algeria. The death toll was 1,138, including 1,015 American troops—the greatest loss of forces at sea in US history. It was also the first successful attack on a ship at sea by a German missile. To keep the news of Germany's new weapon secret and to stop public panic, the US government kept quiet about the tragedy.

PROPAGANDA

In wartime, all governments try to put out messages that help build support for the war effort and maintain morale. This is called propaganda. In World War II, governments used the latest mass media, such as radio and newsreels, to ensure that their propaganda reached as many people as possible. Propaganda often hides or distorts the truth; sometimes it is deliberately false.

PUBLIC ENLIGHTENMENT

Most propaganda in Nazi Germany was produced by the Ministry for Public Enlightenment and Propaganda, run by Joseph Goebbels, who once said, "If you tell a lie, tell a big one." The ministry controlled all the country's media outlets. It fed the German people a constant diet of messages through speeches, posters, newspapers, radio broadcasts, and newsreels.

Germans were continually reminded of their country's ongoing struggle against their enemies, especially the communists and the Jews. They were told of the greatness of German achievements.

This German propaganda poster from World War II intended to raise public morale with the message *"Ein Kampf, ein Sieg!"*— "One fight, one victory!"

British forces arrest William Joyce, the most famous of the Lord Haw-Haws, in Germany at the end of the war. He was hanged for treason in 1946.

When World War II began, most US citizens were firmly against their country becoming involved. US government propaganda focused on convincing people that German and Japanese aggression was a threat to the United States. After the Japanese attack on the US naval base at Pearl Harbor in December 1941, the public no longer needed convincing of this. Propaganda then turned to encouraging people to increase production and conserve resources for the war effort.

The British were described as cowards and Americans as gangsters. German workers were urged to increase their productivity to help with the war effort.

LORD HAW-HAW

Germany even broadcast radio messages in English aimed at people in Britain and the United States. The announcer was known as "Lord Haw-Haw." Several announcers were used, but the most famous was an American named William Joyce. Lord Haw-Haw gave discouraging reports of high Allied losses and called on the British to surrender.

IN THEIR OWN WORDS

Winston Churchill, Britain's wartime prime minister, was famous for his stirring speeches to the nation on the radio. He helped to raise spirits and give hope. Even so, he admitted that lies were sometimes necessary to protect the truth. He said:

In wartime, truth is so precious that she should always be attended by a bodyguard of lies.

DEADLY SECRETS

The worst of all World War II's secrets remained mostly hidden until the war was nearly over. Many people knew about the labor camps to which thousands of Jews and others were sent. Rumors spread about the bad conditions there, but it was only when the first camps were liberated in late 1944 that the world began to learn the full horror of the Holocaust: the Nazi attempt to exterminate the Jews of occupied Europe.

As early as 1933, the Nazis began their anti-Jewish campaign in Germany, preventing the public from patronizing Jewish shops.

HATRED OF JEWS

This mass murder of about six million Jews and the attempt to wipe out Jewish culture in Europe had its roots long before World War II. Hitler's Nazi Party blamed the Jews for all of Germany's problems, including the Great Depression. When they came to power in 1933, the Nazis brought in anti-Jewish laws, and Jews became increasingly isolated from German life. Attacks on Jews increased.

IN THEIR OWN WORDS

Lilli Kopecky, a Jew from Slovakia who survived Auschwitz (one of the death camps), later wrote:

I recall a Dutch Jew asking angrily, "Where is my wife? Where are my children?" The Jews in the barracks said to him, "Look at the chimney [of the crematorium]. They are up there." But the Dutch Jew cursed them . . . This is the greatest strength of the whole crime, its unbelievability.

Quoted in Martin Gilbert, *Never Again* (HarperCollins, 2000)

THE FINAL SOLUTION

When the war began, SS troops followed the German army into conquered territories. They isolated Jewish communities in ghettos. In the Soviet Union, they killed them. In 1941, Nazi leaders decided on the "final solution to the Jewish question." They ordered the building of death camps.

Jews from all over Europe were sent by cattle train to these camps. On arrival, elderly people and children were exterminated in gas chambers and their bodies were burned. The rest were used as slave labor and worked to death. In all, seven out of every 10 Jews living in Europe were murdered in the Holocaust.

LEAVING EVIDENCE

Some Jewish prisoners tried to leave evidence of the Holocaust in case people later found it hard to believe it had happened. At one camp, a buried note was found after the war. It said:

Dear finder, search everywhere, in every inch of soil. Dozens of documents are buried under it . . . Great quantities of teeth are also buried here. It was we . . . who expressly have strewn them all over the terrain . . . so that the world should find material traces of the millions of murdered people.

Quoted in Martin Gilbert, *Never Again* (HarperCollins, 2000)

A German woman is overcome as she walks past the bodies of some 800 slave workers murdered by SS guards. The bodies were laid here by the post-war government so that local people could view the work of their Nazi leaders.

SECRET HIDING PLACES

As the Nazis rounded up Jews across Europe and sent them to the camps, many families went into hiding. Some went into forests; others hid in cellars or secret spaces inside buildings. They all feared the knock on the door in the middle of the night from the Gestapo.

ANNE FRANK

One of the million Jewish children who died in the Holocaust was a German girl named Anne Frank. She and her family moved to Amsterdam, Holland, when the Nazis came to power in 1933. After the Nazi occupation of Holland in 1940, life became increasingly dangerous, and in 1942, they went into hiding.

IN THEIR OWN WORDS

In her diary, Anne Frank wrote:

The Annex is an ideal place to hide in. It may be damp and lopsided, but there's probably not a more comfortable hiding place in all of Amsterdam.

July 11, 1942

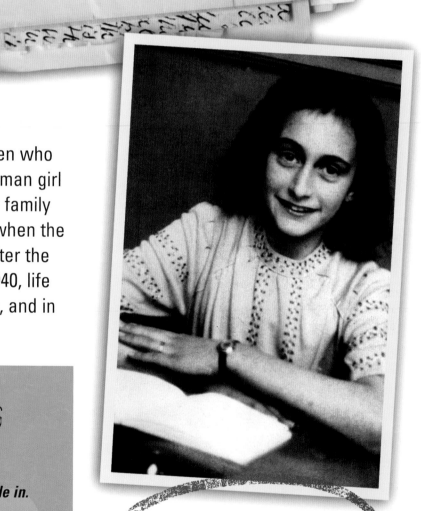

Anne Frank was born on June 12, 1929, and went into hiding when she was 13. She died at the age of 15.

40

In August 1944, someone reported their presence there to the Gestapo and they were arrested. Anne and her sister, Margot, were sent to Belsen camp. They both died there of typhus in March 1945 just a few weeks before British troops arrived to liberate the camp. Otto Frank, Anne's father, survived the war and arranged for her diary to be published. Today her book has been printed in many languages and studied in schools around the world. Hers is the lasting voice of all who died in the Holocaust.

Anne wrote in her diary: "Now our Secret Annex has truly become secret . . . Mr. Kugler thought it would be better to have a bookcase built in front of the entrance to our hiding place. It swings out on its hinges and opens like a door."

For the next two years, they lived in a secret annex of an office, which they shared with another family. Anne's father's friends smuggled food to them, at great risk to themselves. Anne kept a record of her life in the annex in a diary. She wrote about her experiences in hiding, her fears and hopes.

BRONIA BEKER

Bronia Beker was a Jewish girl from Kosowa, Poland. When the Germans invaded in 1941, two of Bronia's brothers, along with many other Jewish men, were taken to a forest and shot. The rest of Bronia's family dug a large cave in the ground where they hid. The Nazis found the cave's ventilation pipes and blocked them up. By the time a friend discovered them, the whole family was dead except for Bronia. She went into hiding on a farm and managed to survive the war.

FINAL SECRETS

As Allied forces closed in on Berlin, Hitler refused to surrender. Instead, he and his most trusted officers and staff retreated to his bunker—a secret complex of underground rooms beneath the city. His last weeks were spent there and have since become the subject of rumor and mystery.

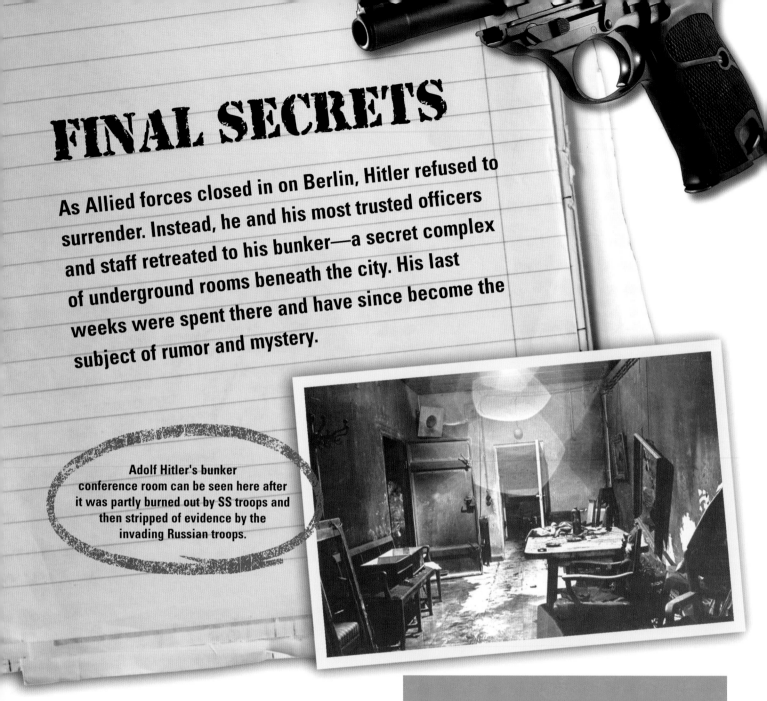

Adolf Hitler's bunker conference room can be seen here after it was partly burned out by SS troops and then stripped of evidence by the invading Russian troops.

HITLER'S FATE

Rumors spread after the war that Hitler had escaped the bunker and survived. The mystery was fueled by the lack of a body and the secrecy of the Soviet authorities following their capture of East Berlin. However, the accepted view now is that Hitler committed suicide in his bunker.

IN THEIR OWN WORDS

On April 20, 1945, Joseph Goebbels toasted Hitler on his 56th birthday. He said:

It is on this beautiful day that we celebrate the Führer's birthday and thank him for he is the only reason why Germany is still alive today.

Ten days later, Hitler was dead and the war in Europe was over.

Major Bernd von Freytag-Loringhoven, a witness to Hitler's last days, later reported that the Führer had become like a sick, old man. By this time, he had lost all grasp of military reality, issuing orders for counterattacks against Allied forces that had no chance of being carried out. He flew into frequent rages, believing he had been betrayed by his generals and his closest colleagues.

Only at the very end did Hitler realize his fate and accept that the Third Reich, which he once said would last 1,000 years, was doomed. On April 29, he married his longtime companion Eva Braun. The following day, with Soviet forces just 1,600 feet (500 meters) from the bunker entrance, he committed suicide.

WHAT HAPPENED TO HIS BODY?

According to the accepted version of events, Hitler and his wife swallowed cyanide pills before he shot himself. Their bodies were then taken to a small garden at ground level and set alight. A Russian museum has exhibited a fragment of bone, which they claim is all that remains of Hitler's skull, but the final resting place of his ashes remains a mystery.

In 1964, this picture was found, apparently taken by a member of Hitler's staff. It supposedly shows Hitler's corpse in his underground bunker.

ESCAPED NAZIS

After the war, many leading Nazis were tried for war crimes at Nuremberg, Germany. However, many more fled Europe and found refuge in Spain, Argentina, Chile, Paraguay, and Brazil. Nazi hunters such as Simon Wiesenthal tried to bring former Nazis accused of war crimes to justice. In a few cases, such as Sebastian Wiemann and Adolf Eichmann, they succeeded. However, many other notorious figures have never been found.

TIMELINE

September 1, 1939 Germany invades Poland, sparking World War II.

August 15, 1941 Josef Jakobs, a German spy, is shot by firing squad at the Tower of London.

October 18, 1941 Richard Sorge, a Soviet spy, is arrested in Tokyo.

December 7, 1941 Japan attacks Pearl Harbor. The United States enters the war.

January 20, 1942 The Wannsee Conference confirms plans for the mass murder of Jews.

June 13, 1942 The Office of Strategic Services (OSS), a US intelligence agency, is founded.

December 1942 Eddie Chapman—Agent Zigzag—a German spy, offers his services to MI5.

April 16, 1943 SOE operative Odette Sansom is arrested and imprisoned.

November 26, 1943 The *Rohna* is sunk with the loss of over 1,000 lives. The news is kept secret.

March 24, 1944 76 Allied prisoners escape from the German prison camp Stalag Luft III.

June 6, 1944 Operation Jedburgh: British and US spies arrive in France to help the Resistance.

June 10, 1944 SOE agent Violette Szabo is captured by German troops.

July 20, 1944 Operation Valkyrie: the attempt to kill Hitler at his Wolf's Lair headquarters fails.

August 4, 1944 Anne Frank and her family are discovered and arrested.

September 7, 1944 The first V-2 is fired—at Paris. The following day, a V-2 hits London.

April 30, 1945 Hitler commits suicide in his bunker. Two days later, Germany surrenders.

September 2, 1945 Japan surrenders and World War II comes to an end.

GLOSSARY

Allies The military and political alliance that fought the Axis powers in World War II, including the United States, Britain, and the Soviet Union.

atom The smallest part into which an element can be divided and still retain its properties.

Axis The military and political alliance of Germany, Italy, and Japan that fought the Allies in World War II.

concentration camp A prison camp used for confining political prisoners, foreign nationals or civilians during wartime.

crematorium A building containing a furnace where bodies are burned.

cyanide A very poisonous chemical that can kill in minutes.

D-day June 6, 1944, the day Allied forces landed in northern France to begin the liberation of occupied Europe in World War II.

Führer The title given to Adolf Hitler, meaning "leader" or "guide" in German.

George Cross The highest gallantry award in the United Kingdom for civilians or military personnel for actions not on the battlefield.

Gestapo The secret police of Nazi Germany. *Gestapo* is a contraction of *Geheime Staatspolizei*: Secret State Police.

ghetto An area of a city lived in by a minority group, whether by choice or because they are forced to.

Home Guard A defense organization of volunteers in the UK during World War II.

intelligence Information, often secret, about an enemy's forces and plans.

internee A civilian who is confined in a prison or concentration camp during a war.

Kempeitai The military police of the Imperial Japanese Army from 1881 to 1945.

Nazi Party The extreme nationalist and racist party that ruled Germany from 1933 to 1945.

newsreels Short news and documentary films shown in movie theaters that were popular during the first half of the 20th century.

nucleus The central part of an atom, consisting of protons and neutrons.

nuclear fission The splitting of the nucleus of an atom.

OVRA The Organization for Vigilance and Repression of Anti-Fascism was the secret police of Italy from 1927 until 1945.

propaganda Information and publicity put out by a government to promote a policy, idea, or cause.

radioactive Describes an element that emits energy in the form of streams of particles due to the decaying of its unstable atoms.

RAF Britain's Royal Air Force.

Soviet Union A state encompassing Russia and other nearby countries, which existed from 1922 to 1991.

Special Operations Executive (SOE) A British organization of World War II responsible for organizing and encouraging espionage and sabotage in occupied Europe.

SS Schutzstaffel, or defense squadron, was a powerful armed force in Nazi Germany known for its brutality.

Third Reich The rule of the Nazi Party in Germany between 1933 and 1945.

treason The crime of attempting to overthrow or harm the government of one's country.

typhus A severe disease and high fever, spread especially by body lice.

U-boat A German military submarine, especially one used during World Wars I and II.

FURTHER INFORMATION

BOOKS

Bruchac, Joseph. *Code Talker: A Novel about the Navajo Marines of World War II*. Puffin Books, 2006.

Frank, Anne. *The Diary of a Young Girl*. Reissue edition: Penguin, 2007.

O'Shei, Tim. *World War II Spies*. Edge Books, 2008.

Ross, Stewart. *At Home in World War II: Propaganda*. Evans Brothers, 2004.

Shapiro, Stephen and Forrester, Tina. *Stories from World War II: Ultra Hush-Hush: Espionage and Special Missions*. Annick Press, 2005.

Walker, Kate and Argaet, Elaine. *Spies and Spying: Super Spies of World War II*. Smart Apple Media, 2003.

WEBSITES

www.annefrank.org

www.historylearningsite.co.uk/WORLD%20WAR%20TWO.htm

www.iwm.org.uk

www.spartacus.schoolnet.co.uk/2WWsecret.htm

INDEX

Page numbers in **bold** refer to illustrations.